LITTLE BOOK OF
CANAL BOATS

LITTLE BOOK OF
CANAL BOATS

First published in the UK in 2013

© Demand Media Limited 2013

www.demand-media.co.uk

All rights reserved. No part of this work may be reproduced or utilised in any form or by any means, electronic or mechanical, including photocopying, recording or by any information storage and retrieval system, without prior written permission of the publisher.

Printed and bound in China

ISBN 978-1-909217-39-3

The views in this book are those of the author but they are general views only and readers are urged to consult the relevant and qualified specialist for individual advice in particular situations.

Demand Media Limited hereby exclude all liability to the extent permitted by law of any errors or omissions in this book and for any loss, damage or expense (whether direct or indirect) suffered by a third party relying on any information contained in this book.

All our best endeavours have been made to secure copyright clearance for every photograph used but in the event of any copyright owner being overlooked please address correspondence to Demand Media Limited, Waterside Chambers, Bridge Barn Lane, Woking, Surrey, GU21 6NL.

Contents

Introduction

Today, the British inland waterway network covers more than 4,000 miles of man–made canals and navigable rivers that not so long ago were part of a much larger system whose tentacles touched nearly all corners of the country. With towpath walks stretching for miles following not only canals that have been the subject of restoration but also those arteries, once important but long since abandoned, there is much to see and do providing all manner of interests to different people.

Many will be attracted to the still and quiet waters simply for the solitude, isolation or the abundance of wildlife so quintessential to the canal landscape. Others will take enormous satisfaction and enjoyment from navigating forgotten backwaters, conveying them out amongst open fields, across windswept moorland and through beautiful vistas aboard vessels representative of another era.

And then there are those who marvel at the utilitarian yet graceful architecture of renovated warehouses, keepers' cottages, locks and aqueducts serving towns and cities that in Victorian times would have reverberated to the sounds of factories, mills and furnaces. Without mile after mile of canals connecting these ever sprawling conurbations during 18th Century, the Industrial Revolution that shaped Britain into a nation of vast wealth might never have happened.

With the cessation of war in 1945, many who in the preceding five or so years had been restrained by the shackles austerity measures had imposed, set about rooting out and saving those elements that once made Britain great. With an overriding feeling of sadness, sentimental nostalgia and despair, they could see the ways of life from a bygone age rapidly disappearing. Tom Rolt and Robert Aickman were amongst the most prominent instigators and in 1946 founded the Inland Waterways Association, an organisation whose primary aim was to conserve the remnants of Britain's canals and navigable rivers that formed such an intrinsic part of the country's economic heritage.

For the industrialists of the 1700s, it was an enormous task building a canal and there were many challenges, obstacles and setbacks to overcome. In writing this book, I hope I have given a brief insight into life on the waterways during the heyday of commercial operation as well as a look at how they have been adapted for today's leisure market.

In some of the chapters, I have focussed on particular examples of civil engineering that are still in daily use thanks in no small part to the dedicated bands of enthusiasts always willing to lend a hand in the restoration of such landmarks. It is because of the sheer effort and time dedicated by such

INTRODUCTION

Above: *Modern fibreglass 'cruiser' type narrow boat, Zena, under construction in 1997*

Centre: *Zena was owned for five or so years by Paul and Diana Woods, the author's in-laws.*

individuals that the rest of us can gaze in awe at these engineering wonders of the Georgian and Victorian period, whilst enjoying the peace and tranquillity of the surrounding countryside. The popularity of holidaying by boat has, since the 1960s, grown to enormous proportions with close to 30,000 vessels registered by British Waterways today.

I would like to show my wholehearted appreciation to the following for their assistance in putting this book together:

Jeremy Beresford; Peter Clews; Tom Marshall; and Ken Warden; to Paul and Diana Woods for allowing me access to

LITTLE BOOK OF **CANAL BOATS**

the log books, diaries and photo records of their extensive trips aboard *Zena* – an early example of an all-fibreglass construction narrow boat – as well as many pleasant hours joining them on their navigations along the Kennet & Avon and River Thames; and finally to my Mum and Dad who probably do not realise just how important the teas, lunches, invaluable use of their conservatory and endless words of encouragement are to me.

Thank you all for your help.

Steve Lanham 2013

Above: *The brand new Zena is lifted into the Kennet & Avon canal at Newbury in 1997*

Taming Britain's Waterways

Before the advent of the railways and the ease with which a network of steel rails could convey goods and passengers across country at great speeds, most travellers relied on the rutted and unpaved roads to get about. In the days before roads were properly metalled, large waggons pulled by strings of horses would churn up the surface so that in times of inclement weather, these routes would become muddy, flooded and often impassable.

Many of Britain's largest inland towns and cities had usually prospered because of their location at a suitable bridging point on a major river. As the condition of highways and byways continued to deteriorate, businesses, small industries and the town's people took to using waterborne craft for the transportation of raw materials, minerals and essential goods.

As far back as the 2nd Century AD, the Romans had realised the potential of canals to link their more established centres of commerce. It is generally understood that around AD 120, the first such waterway in Britain was excavated between Torksey on the River Trent and the city of Lincoln on the River Witham. Stretching for 11½ miles, Fossdyke must at the time have been an extraordinary feat of engineering, not least for the fact that it was dug entirely by hand and without the use of mechanised equipment.

Left: *Fossdyke*

At around the same time an even more ambitious channel, Car Dyke, was begun forging a course through the Lincolnshire countryside and by joining up with other similar arteries, providing a continuous watercourse from Peterborough to York, much of which skirted the edge of the Fens. It was first thought that this system may well have been intended to drain surrounding farmland but there is strong evidence to suggest small cargo vessels navigated the route to supply goods to settlements and Roman Army garrisons it passed along its journey north. Possibly due to Car Dyke's extraordinary length and the manpower required to maintain the banks, it fell into disrepair during the 12th Century and many sections are now silted up completely.

Fossdyke on the other hand was only 11½ miles long and in 1121 was the subject of remedial work by order of King Henry I. In Medieval times there were a number of schemes designed to improve the navigation of rivers especially as they were an ideal solution to the movement of large stone blocks from quarries to the building sites of castles and monasteries. But the importance of Fossdyke as a link to the Trent and a vital trade route was only realised by the people of Lincoln in the 1600s. Samuel Fortey was commissioned to oversee a complete restoration and look into improving the junction at

Torksey where the river is tidal and prone to flooding the surrounding land. In 1672 a sluice-type lock was installed providing a more reliable interchange between the two waterways.

Exeter Ship Canal

One of Britain's oldest mad-made waterways to be built since the Roman occupation was the Exeter Ship Canal completed during the 1560s to link the city's docks to the sea.

For centuries, Exeter was an affluent and strategic trading port with vessels sailing up the estuary in order to deposit their cargos. In the late 1200s, Isabella de Fortibus Countess of Devon, decided to build a weir across the River Exe to provide power to her mills and in doing so blocked access to the docks! In fact it was the establishment of this unfortunate landmark that gave rise to the name Countess Wear, today a suburb on the south-eastern side of the city. Naturally, this caused much opposition and the weir was removed within ten years of its completion. Nevertheless, arrant selfishness appeared to run in the family and in 1317, de Fortibus' cousin, Hugh de Courtenay had constructed another weir and although he had provided a quay downstream at Topsham to allow ships to unload their merchandise – a seemingly magnanimous gesture at the time – de Courtney exploited the

shipping operators and levied heavy tolls for the privilege. Once again, through the greed of a wealthy landowner, the city of Exeter had lost lucrative overseas markets and over the next two centuries its people strongly protested to the monarchy. It was not until the mid-1500s that their remonstrations were taken seriously but for the Exe, it was too little too late. For 250 years, silt from the tributaries that fed into the Exe high up on Exmoor had filtered down the river and, above de Courtenay's weir, the waterway had become un-navigable.

In 1563, John Trew, a Glamorgan engineer was tasked with the construction of a shipping link between a proposed new city dock and the river. For his efforts it was agreed that Trew would be paid the princely sum of £225 plus a regular income from the canal levies. Whilst £225 may sound scant reward for such a job, by today's standards it would amount to well over £750,000. Trew chose to site the entrance to his waterway at a point just below the Countess's original weir and in just over two years the Exeter Ship Canal opened for business.

During the 1600s the canal was extended, dredged to accommodate ships of deeper draught and the number of locks reduced to minimise journey time.

Another hundred years passed before an ambitious scheme was started to

provide an alternative route from the Bristol Channel to Exeter without having to sailing around Land's End. The Grand Western Canal was intended to connect the Ship Canal, via Taunton and Tiverton, to the River Parrett at the Somerset town of Bridgewater, northeast of Exeter and some forty miles away as the crow flies. By 1814 an isolated stretch that meandered its way from Tiverton through the western end of the

Blackdown Hills to Westleigh was open, but creating this 8-mile section alone almost bankrupted the parent company. It was not until 1838 that finances finally allowed the gap to be closed between Westleigh and Bridgewater but, for Exeter, things had once again already moved on. Only nine years before, the Liverpool & Manchester Railway had celebrated its inaugural service and in the following twelve months recorded

carrying more than 450,000 passengers. Rail travel was smooth, fast and a single locomotive could haul a far greater payload in a train than any canal barge could ever hope to carry. Railways were the future and the plans to join the southern end of the Grand Western to Exeter Docks were unceremoniously consigned to the wastepaper basket.

Throughout its 500-year history there were numerous failed attempts to forge better transport links from Exeter to the rest of the country's network and although the Ship Canal has remained an isolated system, its significance in waterways history is assured as it was the very first anywhere in Britain to feature pound-type locks with gates at either end.

Although the railways proved most detrimental to trade on the Ship Canal, a sizeable amount of goods were brought up to the docks in Exeter even as late as the 1970s. In recent times, the basin beside the city's quay was used to moor exhibits from the Maritime Museum. Founded in the late-1960s, it aimed to educate local school children about Exeter's nautical heritage as well as introduce tourism to the area. In 1998, however, the Museum closed and many of the exhibits were dispersed to other localities around the country. Today, the quayside only attracts visiting leisure craft cruising along the south Devonshire coast and the English Channel.

Bridgewater Canal

Whilst the Exeter Ship Canal was an attempt to rejuvenate trade along the route of an existing waterway, the Bridgewater Canal holds it place in British history as the first to be built over land largely where there was no previous natural watercourse. It was the brainchild of Francis Egerton, the 3rd Duke of Bridgewater who had earlier toured extensively on the Continent and saw for himself how European engineers were already embracing the concept of transporting large quantities of minerals

Above: *In 1971, the Bridgewater Canal broke its banks at Bollin Aqueduct and it was two years before the waterway was reopened*

by canal. So impressed was Egerton that in 1759 (and at the tender age of 24) he was granted Royal approval to begin digging not only a link east to the River Irwell at Salford, but also south-west to the Mersey at Warrington, in effect expanding potential markets from his well-established collieries at Worsley Delph. The shrewd Egerton also realised that by providing a cross-country transport route, those industries established in close proximity to the canal would see the benefits of using the system for their own needs and would happily pay a toll to do so.

The mines at Worsley consisted of a myriad of man-made subterranean waterways which astonishingly totalled over 45 miles in length. Incredibly, once inside and having navigated further into the caverns, 12-ton barges called 'starvationers' would then descend to a depth level with the coal seams via an underground inclined plane – an innovation designed by John Gilbert. So rich were the seams in this area that the Worsley underground colliery continued coal production right up to the late-1800s.

Earl Gower, the Duke's brother-in-law and something of a magnate within the pottery industry was also looking to construct a separate canal between the Rivers Trent and Mersey and so whilst work continued, the two parties pooled their ideas and the plans were revised. Concentrating only on the Salford route, the canal was altered and instead extended across the Irwell via a stone aqueduct at Barton before terminating for the time being at Stretford. The work took two years to complete with the official opening taking place in July 1761. By 1765, its easternmost tentacle had reached the industrial heart of Manchester with a new basin excavated at Castlefield. Forty years later, this site would form the south-western end of the Rochdale Canal, a tortuous 32-mile system connecting Manchester with Sowerby Bridge, comprising 91 locks, and the first of three canals to cross the Pennines.

It had always been the Duke of Bridgewater's intention, however, to link his collieries with the great port of Liverpool and as early as 1762, attention had turned to forging a further waterway that instead of running north of the Irwell as had been previously planned, took a route from Stretford south through Sale and then west passing Altrincham, Lymm and Warrington before approaching the Mersey at Runcorn. This was not without its geographical headaches and aqueducts built over the Mersey at Sale and over the Bollin between Dunham Town and Little Bollington, as well as a major flight of ten locks required to bring the canal down to sea level at Runcorn, meant this formidable 23-mile undertaking endured for the next fourteen years. It also led to near bankruptcy for the Duke who had injected a sizeable fortune into the project.

Despite financial setbacks, he was determined to expand the transport arteries around Greater Manchester and in 1795 work began on yet another canal from Worsley, this time stretching some 5½ miles west to Leigh. Eventually the Leeds & Liverpool Canal would also build a branch into Leigh from Wigan and connect up with the Bridgewater, and this arm was completed in 1820. Unfortunately the Duke was not around to see this momentous achievement as he had passed away some seventeen years before. Nevertheless, through his foresight and perseverance, he had helped to create an uninterrupted trade route between the north of England, Greater Manchester, Liverpool, and most importantly lucrative markets overseas.

So convenient and successful was the Bridgewater system that it continued in commercial operation until 1974, far later than most of the other systems around the country. During the late 1800s, it had been purchased by the Manchester Ship Canal Company and today, the waterway is still managed by same parent group with the Bridgewater Canal Trust ensuring its historical significance is preserved for the education and enjoyment of future generations.

The back-breaking job of actually building the country's canals was assigned to teams of men called 'navvies', a term first coined in the late-18th Century and derived literally from the word 'navigator'. Navvies were specialists in their field methodically clearing the intended route of trees, soil and rock by hand with rarely more than just saws, picks and shovels. Predominantly uneducated and illiterate, these immensely strong and hardened individuals were recruited from all over Britain with a significant number coming over the Irish Sea or from across the Scottish border to seek employment. They lived in temporary shanty towns and as the monumental task progressed, so the ramshackle array of tents and wooden huts would periodically be relocated.

Few women lived on site and navvies had a notorious reputation for fighting not only with the inhabitants from the surrounding villages but also between themselves, no doubt triggered by an argument concerning the fairer sex, though more often than not fuelled by excessive inebriation! Nevertheless, once a waterway was complete, this rowdy bunch of rogues would migrate to wherever another system was under construction – much to a collective sigh of relief from the native population as well as the local constabulary!

Many people might romanticise about living on a narrow boat, but the fact remains that life on the canals in Georgian and Victorian times was typically demanding, arduous and poorly paid, and villagers residing close to the waterways would regard families who lived on the canal with the same level of disdain and contempt as they did with the navvies.

Right: *Canal Dredger*

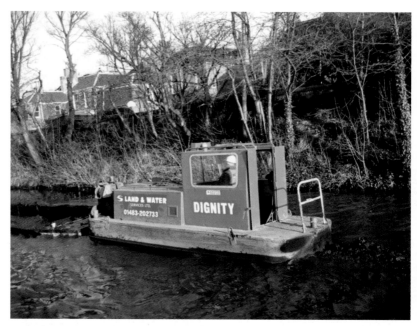

Forever at one with the elements, the winter months were cold and dark whilst the summer heat was often unbearable. There were of course times when the weather was calm, clear and warm and must have been a delight to work in but whatever the conditions, come rain or shine, deliveries had to be made.

Harsh winter freezes caused the greatest loss of business and it was not uncommon for canal traffic to come to a standstill when vessels not strong enough to plough their own course through a frozen channel were left icebound. To prevent this happening too many times, ice breaking narrow boats were specially built with toughened bows to create a safe, continuous and usable route. Dredging barges were used so that all systems were kept free of weed, silt or discarded items that could foul a boat's rudder or propeller. In addition, a whole army of staff were employed all year round to ensure tolls and mooring fees were paid, locks were maintained in working order, and the canal-side flora and fauna was managed and regularly cut back.

The main reason for preventing bushes and trees from growing on the banks was to stop tow ropes snagging – a serious consideration that could result in disaster. Records show that occasionally a rope would become entangled in an object at the canal-side, and as the heavy barge continued forward, so the taught rope would drag the hapless tow horse backwards and into the water.

Working barges had no brakes to speak of and with a maximum payload weighing in excess of 35 tonnes, would invariably travel a long way before slowing to a standstill. The only effective ways of stopping such a vessel within a short distance was either to steer it into the bank thus risking damage to the hull, or lasso a line tied to the barge around one of the 'strapping posts' – vertical wooden or iron stakes driven into the ground at regular intervals along the sides of the waterway.

A Town Born out of a Canal

Far Right:
Caldwall Lock near Kidderminster on the Staffordshire & Worcestershire Canal

Once upon a time, there was a village called Lower Mitton that lay nestled between the confluence of the Rivers Severn and Stour. Right up to the late-18th Century, there was nothing out of the ordinary about this sleepy little hamlet other than over time it had slowly established itself on a direct highway and roughly half way between Hereford and Birmingham. It also served as a brief stopping off point for the shallow draught vessels making their way to the northernmost navigable section of the Severn at Bewdley where their cargos were unloaded and taken on to Birmingham by road.

But in 1766, many of the residents may have been surprised and rather curious to see a gentleman who went by the name of James Brindley, taking measurements and making calculations of the land north of the village and generally following a route west of the Stour. Those who had any knowledge and interest in British civil engineering, however, would undoubtedly have heard of him as he was one of this country's greatest canal surveyors and designers.

Brindley continued his analysis along the valley towards Kidderminster where his exploration took him across the river and, from there, north past Wolverhampton and Stafford. His plan was to build a transport artery to link the River Severn to Great Haywood,

some 4½ miles east of Stafford where another system, the Trent & Mersey, was under construction. When the project received Royal approval in 1767 work began almost immediately and within only three years, the first sections were ready for use. It was not until 1772 that to much fanfare, the Staffordshire & Worcestershire Canal was opened fully. Its excavation, having

cost a total of £100,000, had carved a path right through the middle of Lower Mitton. It would prove to be Brindley's last project as, in that same year, he died of diabetes exacerbated in all likelihood by his dedication to the job at hand.

The 1770s were the golden age of canal expansion especially around Birmingham. A spaghetti-like network quickly spread throughout the Black

Country area and with them lucrative nationwide trading possibilities for any industry centred on a canal system. Lower Mitton was ideally place for passing trade such as coal from Staffordshire, clay products from the Potteries, timber locally felled in the Wyre Forest, iron ore from Gloucestershire, and most importantly goods brought from overseas into the great seaport at Bristol.

There were boat builders and repair shops along the river and canal sides, and the depth of the channel in the Severn allowed tall-masted trows to be brought up from Gloucester and Bristol and exchange cargos with the narrow boats. Indeed, as the Stour was one of the most inland points to which trows could navigate, the land that Lower

Mitton once occupied soon became known as Stour Port.

Five years after the canal's opening, its most northerly end was linked up with the new Trent & Mersey Canal via the junction at Great Haywood providing the most direct watercourse between Liverpool and Bristol. In 1779, the Stourbridge Canal closed the gap between the Staffordshire & Worcestershire and another system, the Dudley Canal built nine years earlier, and most importantly gave access to collieries in and around Tipton.

Once the first basin had been established at Stour Port, it took little time before it was surrounded by newly-erected factories and mills and by the mid-1780s, there were businesses manufacturing carpets, textiles, leather, and brass and iron ware. With the new Century came additional traffic, four more basins were opened to cope with the expansion and to speed up the transfer of boats from the canal to the Severn, new sets of locks were installed.

As more and more workers moved in to the area in search of employment, small traders set up domestic goods shops to cater for the growing population. A pumping house was also built in 1806 and furnished with a stationary steam-driven beam engine forged in the Soho foundry of Boulton & Watt, a Birmingham company specialising in this field of technology. The Stour Port engine drew river water from the Severn to replenish the higher canal level north of the town and when working at full tilt was capable of shifting 160,000 gallons every hour.

In 1815 yet another system opened, the Worcester & Birmingham, creating a direct route between those two cities. A year later this linked up with the Stratford-upon-Avon Canal which, in turn, connected to the Grand Union at Lapworth. As Worcester was twelve miles downstream on the Severn, this had a dramatic and detrimental effect on Stourport and over the next fifty years industries around the basins gradually went into decline.

Even the Shropshire Union that in 1835 made a connection with the Staffordshire & Worcestershire at Wolverhampton could not save the fortunes of the town and when the Severn Valley Railway was built from Shrewsbury in 1862, its route dictated that Stourport would only be served by

a branch off the main line to Worcester.

One of the first major signs that things were looking even bleaker for the future of the town's canal was when a basin in the Cheapside district was filled in and the land used for a new gas works. Nevertheless, there were still a handful of industries that right up to the 1940s stayed loyal to the Staffordshire and Worcestershire, with cargo vessels making regular deliveries to the likes of Cadbury at Bourneville and the Royal Worcester potteries. A new power station had opened in 1927 throwing

the canal a life line with weekly consignments of coal being brought south from the collieries at Cannock Chase. But that all ended in 1949 when the final boatload marked the last time this particular waterway would be used for commercial traffic.

In the decades following World War II, Stourport lost much of its industry including the gasworks which also ceased operation in 1949 and the Lichfield basin which was filled in a year later. Even in fairly recent times, employment prospects have been hit by further significant losses. In Cheapside, a vinegar brewery that had in its latter years become part of the Sarson's brand, closed its doors altogether in 1998 exactly 200 years after it had first commenced business. It looked as though many of the redundant and derelict warehouses and foundry buildings would be torn

down to be replaced by office or residential premises. Luckily, some of the most important landmarks around the central basins have remained standing including the Iron Warehouse which dates from 1771, The Tontine (originally the Stourport Inn) of 1773, and the imposing Clock Warehouse built later in the century and so-called because of the clock which was added several years after.

In 2006 work began to restore and develop Stourport's canal district with financial help provided by the Heritage Lottery Fund and British Waterways.

Today, the Staffordshire and Worcestershire Canal is one of the prettiest inland waterways in the country and Stourport acts as the end of many a holiday expedition for those not brave enough to venture further into the upper shallows of the Severn.

Anatomy of a Canal Boat

Working Boats

By the late 18th Century, tentacles of navigable waterways reached far across the British Isles linking from the choked and bustling towns and cities, those great centres of industry, to the sea as well as to important sources of raw material and minerals.

Excavating wide channels across the British countryside would have been a costly business and to minimise expenditure, canals were dug with just enough room for vessels to pass each other or those moored at the waters edge. It is thought that one the greatest waterways engineer, James Brindley, was first to suggest that locks should be built to around 7ft wide and just over 70ft in length. These dimensions might have been calculated bearing in mind that companies could ill afford the expenditure and time of digging deep passages and that a 35 ton payload was deemed the maximum a heavy horse (at that time the only source of motive power) was capable of pulling at walking pace. Nevertheless, this became a standard for many new systems and narrow boats were constructed accordingly. It eventually came to pass that only vessels favoured with particularly shallow draughts would be able to navigate the majority of man-made waterways throughout the Midlands.

With iron and steel hulls not being

introduced until the 19th Century, the first narrow boats were of simple wooden construction, representing little more than open barges with tarpaulins covering their cargos to protect them from inclement weather. These vessels were often handled by a crew of no more than two – one on board at the helm who was also charged with operating the locks, and a second member who remained on land to guide the horse along the tow path, through tunnels and over bridges.

In the event of two horse-drawn boats approaching one another, it was protocol for to stop and wait while the helmsman kept the barge over to the far side of the channel. This had the desired effect that the towing rope went slack and sank to the canal bed, allowing the oncoming horse to step over it and its barge to glide over without snagging. Children were commonly employed to lead horses and were not always averse to the rules, occasionally resulting in some spur-of-the-moment ducking and diving onboard the nearside vessel as the taught rope whipped across at head height!

Over-bridges were installed to carry roads or even the towpath from one side of the canal to the other and the archways were generally constructed to only slightly wider than the width of a narrow boat. This was done to save money on build materials and it was normally acknowledged that the

boat closer to the bridge had the right of way.

Although part and parcel of pre-mechanisation, the use of horses as the main source of motive power created a separate and thriving canal-side industry with blacksmiths shops and stables all playing an important role at strategic overnight rest stops. Many canal companies provided their own facilities as it was essential for the horse to recuperate from a long day's journeying. For the crews of vessels devoid of cabin accommodation

lodgings were made available, but it is no accident that many brewery-owned pubs just happened to open for business besides the canal network at mooring basins and main bridging points.

Joey-Boats and Starvationers

The 'Joey' was a type of wooden hulled horse-drawn vessel peculiar to the Birmingham coal fields. These were a very basic and utilitarian form of workaday narrow boat made unusually with a bow at each end and

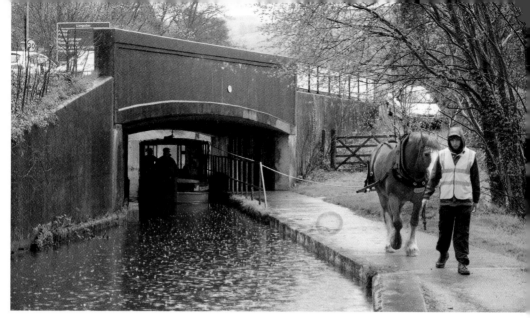

an interchangeable rudder and designed to eliminate any need to turn the vessel around once it had deposited its cargo. This arrangement naturally sped up delivery times and with the collieries situated in close proximity to the city, journeys were kept short and accommodation cabins were not required aboard the boats allowing for maximum coal capacity.

'Starvationers' were similar to 'Joeys' in having two bows. They worked in the Duke of Bridgewater's underground collieries at Worsley

Delph on the outskirts of Manchester. With a maximum capacity of 12 tons, these were somewhat smaller than the open-air barges but were designed to fit into the caissons that descended the inclined plane the Duke had installed within the mine.

As the Industrial Revolution took hold in Britain, mechanical technology developed and with the advent of steam power, a handful of narrow boats were converted to be self-propelled by installing them with small

LITTLE BOOK OF **CANAL BOATS**

marine engines. In time these would be superseded by internal combustion units but by then, businesses were choosing to send freight at much greater speeds on the growing sprawl of roads and railway lines rather than the at a sedate pace around the canal network. Certainly the 20th Century saw British waterways lose most of its trade and by the late-1940s, only one or two were still being used commercially.

There were, however, a great number of unfortunate city folk who during World War II had suffered bombing raids at the hands of the Luftwaffe and many sought shelter in all manner of temporary accommodation. As well as moving into prefab homes and caravans, displaced evacuees were able to purchase narrow boats that had once earned their keep plying the canals carrying minerals, foodstuff or pottery. Bought for a song, these redundant and unloved vessels were converted into relatively comfortable but nevertheless vital living space.

Pleasure Boats

In the decade following the war, ordinary people who had endured those preceding dark days and forced to tolerate austerity measures were once again embracing their vacation and free time, and looked for ways to explore and enjoy the countryside around them. With large stretches of the canal network coming to the attention of restoration groups and volunteers, holidaying by hired narrow boat gradually became a popular pastime – much to the bewilderment of the commercial boat crews who previously had only viewed these cross–country arteries as a place of work.

By the 1960s, boat builders were also realising the potential and tapped into the leisure market as demand grew. As well as the old working boats being modified with new or extended accommodation cabins and furnished with all the essentials for everyday living, the number of new vessels entering the

water increased. Outwardly, these more often than not followed long-established design practice but with the addition of mod-cons to cater for the leisure market.

Today, narrow boats do not come in all shapes exactly, but will certainly differ in sizes – well length anyway – and second-hand boat dealers will offer vessels measuring anything from 20 feet to 70 feet. To some it might seem that all narrow boats on our inland waterways look the same, but there are a few styling variations that separate them into several categories:

The Traditional

As its name suggests, in terms of modern-day leisure craft, the 'traditional' follows (as much as possible) the profile attributed to the original working vessels. The tapered cabin emulates the line of tarpaulins that used

to protect commercial cargos and will usually extend almost the full length of the hull with an open area at the bow end large enough to seat three or four passengers. The 'traditional' will also have a small deck aft of the cabin affording just about enough room for the helmsman and little or nobody else. Immediately forward of this is a doorway giving entry into the living accommodation. In days gone by, this would have been occupied by the steam or diesel engine, but today the units providing motive power are so compact that they can be hidden away below decks and accessed for maintenance purposes from inside through a lifting hatch.

The Semi-Traditional

From a side elevation, the 'semi-traditional' looks almost identical

to the 'traditional' type narrow boat yet benefits from an open-air seating area just forward of the helm. Although this generally precludes several feet of undercover living accommodation, storage lockers are often built under the seats and unlike the 'traditional', there is enough room for all the crew to enjoy the journey whilst sat together.

The Tug

In the late 1800s the horse-drawn barge was gradually replaced by self-propelled vessels, and by the early part of the next century, many operators were exploiting the increase in motive power using tug type narrow boats to pull non-motorised barges (also known as 'dumb' boats or 'butties'). It was an attempt to improve efficiency at a time when railway companies were successfully poaching much of the freight contracts. Initially, the plan worked and hundreds of new vessels were ordered, specifically to operate in pairs. On the Birmingham Canal Navigation, it was easier for a tug to pull more than one barge than on other systems because there were fewer locks for the operating crews to negotiate.

Tugs were often furnished with a covered area for the steam engine and coke storage, and later with sleeping accommodation. Today, a tug style narrow boat is distinguishable by its greater open cockpit area towards the bows. Because of this, they have a somewhat shortened cabin situated aft which most likely explains why there are fewer examples used as residential or holiday boats. A tug will tend to display an old-fashioned workmanlike appearance featuring portholes down the sides rather than the larger rectangular picture windows found on the majority of 'traditional' and 'cruiser' type leisure craft.

The Josher

Perhaps the most successful independent transport firm to make use of the canal network was Fellows, Morton & Clayton. Started in 1837 by James Fellows, they competed with the canal companies for contracts to move huge quantities of bulk goods in and around the Birmingham area.

In 1876, Frederick Morton joined the firm and several years later, Fellows, Morton & Co. amalgamated with a

Far Left: *A nicely restored 'tug' type narrow boat showing ample cargo capacity but only a short cabin*

Above: *A narrow boat painted in the livery of Fellows, Morton & Clayton displaying the 'traditional' style rear deck affording room for the helmsman and little else*

neighbouring bulk carrier, William Clayton of Oldbury. Initially the fleet consisted of only wooden vessels but by 1894, and with business booming, they opportunity arose to invest in new boats featuring long slender hulls of riveted iron. Nicknamed after the company founder's son Joshua who had taken over the reigns during the 1860s, some 'Joshers' were constructed in the company's own boatyards whilst others were put out to tender, but always built to a specific and quite distinctive design. Benefiting from rakish bow lines and high finish quality, Joshers were popular among their crews and became the envy of the competition.

As the 20th Century dawned, F.M. & C were operating a number of steam barges but continued to use horse-drawn dumb boats alongside as they had larger carrying capacity. Just prior to the outbreak of World War I, they took delivery of their first internal combustion engined vessel and over the course of the next twenty years, built up a fleet of around one hundred similar craft.

In 1948, the newly elected Labour Government brought in a program of nationalisation whereby funds received via the profit making industries such as railways, buses, mining, steel production and amenities could be distributed amongst the non-profit making organisations including education, The National Health Service, and the emergency and armed services. As part of a newly centralised transport infrastructure, all canals and navigable rivers were placed under one banner, British Waterways, and Fellows, Morton & Clayton were absorbed into this government department. With much investment earmarked for road and rail improvements, most of the boats from this once proud fleet were retired,

ending their working days rotting away in derelict basins or boat yards. A great many, however, were saved and sold on at a cheap price. With their good handling properties, Joshers proved ideal candidates for conversion into leisure boats as well as providing a blueprint for future vessels.

The Cruiser

At one time there were more 'traditional' craft using the canal than any other, but their numbers have now been overtaken by the more popular and user friendly 'cruiser' type. The main difference between the two is that 'cruisers' have a much more generous deck area at the stern offering space to sit and sip a glass or two when moored up. This is often surrounded by a wooden rail giving the helmsman somewhere to perch and enjoy the scenery as he chugs along between fields and meadows and away from it all. Because of the increased decking aft of the cabin, the marine engine will invariably be located directly below this.

Above: *A modern 'cruiser' type fibreglass narrow boat with larger rear deck and wooden rail*

Above: *Steel hulled 'cruisers'*

Not only will it be the diminutive narrow boat that is found on Britain's canals today, but many small sea-going craft look equally at home on our inland waterways, especially when cruising the lakes and rivers of the Norfolk Broads, for example, where there are fewer low bridges with restricted headroom. Shipping channels and natural waterways deep enough for navigation tend to be much wider than their man-made counterparts and throughout history there has been a tradition of vessels operating along these systems that were built to more generous proportions especially across the beam than the traditional narrow boat.

Short Boats

The 'short boat' was another vessel unique to one particular system and was built to an overall length of just 60 feet but with a width of 14 feet. Their unusual dimensions were dictated by the size of locks through which they operated on located over 92 miles of the Leeds & Liverpool Canal between Leeds and Wigan. The locks had been designed specifically to accommodate 'Keels', a type of vessel that plied its trade along the navigable rivers of Yorkshire, and therefore prevented longer narrow boats of other waterways from using the canal. That legacy continues today although some owners have been known to squeeze slightly longer vessels into the locks but at an angle – a procedure only possible due to the double width chamber between the gates and as long as the bow of the boat does not foul the arc of the tail gate when it opens inwards into the lock.

Long Boats

From Wigan to Manchester, the locks were built to the national standard 72 feet in length but were 14 foot 3 inches wide. Again, this gave rise to another completely separate form of craft called the 'Long Boat' which had one of the largest load carrying capacities

of any inland waterway vessel – the only type longer being the 85 foot coal barges that worked from the Cannock Chase collieries into Birmingham via the Wyrley & Essington Canal.

The Dutch Barge

As the name suggests, this type of vessel was developed in the Netherlands and was used extensively on Dutch inland waterways for carrying bulk goods. Characterised by a wooden and later steel flat-bottomed hull, typically wide beam, and an all-weather wheelhouse protruding above the main cabin, they would have originally operated under sail. The mast and wheelhouse were both collapsible allowing for passage under low bridges but as technology progressed, more and more examples would be fitted with an internal combustion engine rendering the mast virtually redundant.

Today Dutch barges are popular, not only as comfortable and spacious holiday vessels but also for well-proportioned living accommodation and for those reasons alone are very sought after, commanding a premium price whenever they come up for sale.

Right: *The generous proportions of a 'Dutch' type barge are illustrated well in this picture of Golden Thistle*

Sailing Barges, Flats and Wherries

For a number of Britain's navigable rivers and natural waterways, wide beam shallow draught sailing barges were developed. These included the square-rigged flat-bottomed Thames Barges that could operate out of the Docklands area and as far west as Oxford, and the Severn Trows that left the great seaport of Bristol and headed upstream to the Birmingham canal network's transhipment points at Stourport and Worcester.

Mersey Flats served the Duke of Bridgewaters' Worsley Collieries and on entering some of the wider canals and rivers around Liverpool, Cheshire and Greater Manchester, their masts could be lowered if necessary to negotiate low bridges. Other 'flats' were built devoid of masts and sails and were instead pulled by heavy horse. Later, steam driven 'flats' pulling non-powered barges traded out of the salt works between Winsford and Northwich along the Weaver to Liverpool.

The Norfolk Broads are an isolated network of navigable waterways that include wide lakes (hence the name) and connecting rivers that, today, attract thousands of holidaymakers each year. Once again, the leisure industry has only seriously exploited this area of East Anglia since World War II. Up until then, the only craft venturing into these waters on a regular basis were the Norfolk Wherries that traded between Norwich, Great Yarmouth and Lowestoft.

Where the vast majority of working boats lost their industrial integrity in the 1960s and 70s when they were bought up for conversion to leisure craft, a good number escaped and survived in tact. During the post-War period there were many people who enthused about that golden Victorian age when the countries foundries, factories and mills were the envy of the civilised world. They could see how things were quickly changing and set about rescuing what remnants were left. Individuals such as Tom Rolt who, by saving the fortunes of the Talyllyn Railway in mid-Wales was instrumental in launching the railway preservation movement, were adamant that we should conserve these relics from Britain's industrial heritage, not only as a testament to the men who built them, but as educational tools and tourist attractions for future generations to enjoy. Luckily, Rolt was also a canal buff and in the years immediately after World War II would often take jaunts along his local systems. It is thanks in no small part to him and all the dedicated volunteers who followed in his footsteps that we can enjoy the tranquillity and virtual solitude that our waterways provide.

ANATOMY OF A CANAL BOAT

Right: *Roses and castles are very much in evidence on this beautifully restored ex-working narrow boat*

Roses & Castles

During the height of The Industrial Revolution, firms that operated fleets of barges would encourage those men working in the boatyards who displayed a certain flair for sign-writing to paint the company name on the flat sides of a vessel's cabin and, as

intricate and flamboyant, symbolising a great source of pride amongst the workforce. Lettering framed with elaborate scrollwork would be rendered with astonishing skill and precision, and boats from separate regions could often be identified by the style of decoration. Not all canal companies embraced the concept and barge crews navigating the Chesterfield Canal, for example, were steadfastly refused such ostentation.

The tradition of painting romanticised images and ornate patterns on exposed surfaces is thought to have first been adopted in the Midlands, possibly influenced by the fancy pottery transported throughout the region. Comparisons lead others to think it may have originated in Holland, Eastern Europe or, indeed, as far away as Asia. There was once a popular belief that the decoration applied to Romany caravans had simply translated over to the canals and although this theory has since been largely discounted, there are certainly similarities.

The custom most likely began in the mid-1800s when seasoned boatmen who earned their keep transporting cargo on Britain's inland waterways, made their vessels home to their families. It made economic

technology advanced, its engine house. As different concerns vied for trade against an ever looming threat from the railways, the practice spread and the artwork gradually became more

sense to employ only two people to operate a horse-drawn butty – one to steer and the other to look after the horse, and men who were experienced canal workers capable of reading the characteristics of the channel ahead tended to remain at the helm whilst their wives stayed on the towpath. And once they were old enough, the children were taught to perform various tasks in the day to day running, effectively becoming additional but cheap labour. Narrow boats were by their very nature a cramped and utilitarian form of transport but as more and more women took to living onboard, many quite understandably wanted to introduce their own refinements in an attempt to add a certain touch of elegance and home comfort to these otherwise drab little vessels.

Wooden interior panels were adorned with delicate and beautifully painted flowers, landscapes, scenes the family may have encountered on their journey, or picturesque buildings such as churches and castles. In fact the two most popular themes coined the phrase 'Roses & Castles' that, today, is generally used to describe this particular

art movement.

Once the living space had been suitably improved, attention then turned to particular accessories outside. Good use of rest stops were made when everyday items such as buckets, water barrels, ladders and gangplanks were given a fresh coat of paint and

Left: *Modern sign-written lettering and scrollwork continuing an age old tradition on the canals*

embellished with more illustrations. In time, the outer cabin panels, hull sides, tillers and handrails would also receive a similar treatment that, together, provided an attractive and welcome splash of colour amongst the grime and smoke that once choked industrial towns and cities.

Today, the tradition is more popular than ever and although illustrations can be bought in the form of proprietary transfers, there are still dedicated artists and sign-writers up and down the country offering their services and earning a living putting the finishing touches to new or restored canal boats.

Life on the Canal Today

Far Right:
*An array of
waterborne craft
moored up for the
winter*

The Modern Leisure Boat

There are almost 30,000 vessels registered by British Waterways today with the majority comprised of modern steel hulls and cabins. Fibreglass has also been used extensively especially for open-water cruiser type craft but has its drawbacks. When employed for the overall construction of a canal boat, for example, surfaces below the waterline can suffer from osmosis – blistering due to water penetrating through the top protective layer.

Another problem and thankfully less common has not so much to do with the weight or durability of fibreglass, but more to do with its strength combined with the inability of other canal users to navigate their own vessels properly! A steel hulled narrow boat bearing out of control towards one with a fibreglass hull is only going to have one outcome but regulations are set to avoid such disastrous consequences!

The first and probably most important rule to remember is that all canal and river users travelling in opposite directions must pass each other on the right – an international rule observed the world over. Vessels being overtaken should allow the faster boat enough room – preferably on a straight section – to get past by manoeuvring closer to the right-hand bank, whilst on ship canals, it is always

Right: *Modern leisure boats are often well-appointed with all the basic mod-cons of home*

advisable to retreat off the deep water channel when faced with an oncoming freight carrier. Narrow canals are often flanked by reed beds, tree growth and fallen debris and it is quite acceptable to follow a path down the centre line. Observing the maximum speed limit of four miles per hour should always give plenty of time to move to the sides when necessary. Chugging along at a relaxed pace also minimises the risk of waves causing detrimental erosion to the canal beds and banks and subsequently effect the wildlife living there.

The modern leisure boat that navigates our inland waterways is, today, full of gadgetry, mod-cons and an interior that shows little resemblance to its workaday forebear. People holidaying by canal for the first time might be surprised to find their narrow boat benefiting from central heating, satellite TV, a near fully-fitted kitchen with electric hob, oven and refrigerator, a double bed instead of or in addition to bunks, a shower or bath, and even a toilet that flushes (there's progress for you!), in fact all the practical comforts of home shoehorned into a space measuring little more than

six feet wide. With over 4,000 miles of canal to choose from, what better way to tour the country!

The Canal Boat as a Home

Whilst a number of displaced wartime evacuees took to living in narrow boats and other waterborne craft sighting this basic necessity in the hope that it was only temporary accommodation, there are people today who still choose to make these comparatively confined and rudimentary vessels their homes. Owners are required to declare if they intend to keep their boat permanently moored at one location. In such cases, planning permission needs to be sought as it would then count as a houseboat and permanent moorings also incur council tax and levies on amenities such as water and electricity. Alternatively, they can decide to travel the length and breadth of England's waterways, never staying in one place for more than a fortnight, and anyone considering this course of action might be wise to take particular care when selecting his or her craft. A number of variations between the dimensions of locks on different

Right: *Many people choose to live aboard canal boats all year round and enjoy a very Bohemian lifestyle!*

waterways, would mean it would have to be no wider than 6 foot 10 inches and no more than 60 foot in length to negotiate all the existing navigable and restored canal systems that connect into today's main network.

A typical narrow boat may not be adequately equipped for the temperature drop during the winter months and some modification might be necessary. This may include extra insulation to all walls, the addition of a wood burning stove or another form of better heating.

Where many may struggle to secure financial help when attempting to buy a property on terra firma, it may come as a surprise to some that specialist lenders and even high street banks will provide marine mortgages for vessels costing over £3,000 (as of 2013) with the new purchaser only having to find as little as 30% of the value to secure the craft. For those who need to escape to a quieter life, living on a narrow boat can be an ideal solution and at the time of writing, both fixed rate mortgages of up to a £25,000 loan repaid over 60 months, or variable rate over 5 to 10 years for loans over £25,000 were available.

Locks, Flights & Staircases

For centuries, locks have been used in all parts of the world to transfer commercial cargo carrying vessels from one level of navigable river or man-made canal to another.

Navigable rivers are commonly those which have been improved to accommodate boats with a deeper draught than the original depth of the water and in the 17th Century, there were a number of schemes designed to make untamed watercourses including the Rivers Thames and Wey into safer shipping lanes. This might involve diverting the course of the river, reinforcing banks, or the addition of artificial flood barriers and levees. By introducing weirs at strategic points, a usable channel could be created where before there were only shallows. A weir, however, would then form a step down from one level to the next, and if it was positioned on a fast flowing river, a torrent of water would cascade over it generating potentially dangerous undercurrents. So that a boat could safely enter the lower reaches, a pound lock had to be installed slightly further downstream. River locks were also used to bypass particularly fast flowing sections or stretches of river containing rapids.

By the mid–1700s enough rivers had been upgraded for most of England's population to be within a day's walking distance of an important waterborne trade route. There were also substantial

GILL

canals planned, completed or under construction as the industrial age gripped the nation.

The surveyors who first designed Britain's man-made waterways chose flat low-lying terrain to dig the earliest channels. They were ideal for safely conveying goods for miles without having to negotiate any major obstacles. Later, when civil engineers were tasked with providing cross-country canals, they would try as much as possible to follow a course that kept on a level plane. But if tracing a contour for miles round a hillside meant a ridiculously long deviation from the intended route, then it was far more cost effective to go up and over the hill using a lock, a number of locks, or a 'flight' – a series of consecutive locks in close proximity to one another. On even steeper inclines where there was not enough room for a pound – the navigable stretch of water between any two individual

Above: *A nicely renovated lock keeper's cottage*

Centre: *The giant lock at Limehouse Basin that separates the River Thames from the Regent's Canal (now part of the Grand Union) has rotating lock gate*

locks – a 'staircase' would be required whereby the 'head' gate of the lowest lock constituted as the 'tail' gate of the next lock above, and so on up the rise. The staircase at Bingley, for example, consists of four lock chambers between the upper and lower pounds, separated by just five gates.

As they were specifically intended for the carriage of commodities, raw materials and minerals, canals were required to cover great distances across country, and invariably traversed diverse and undulating terrain. Canal locks were therefore an ingenious way to continue a waterway up or down a steep incline without having to resort to an alternative means to convey the goods.

In the mid-1800s at the height of commercial canal operation, 'keepers' were employed at each major set of locks to open or close the gates. Living in specially built cottages besides the canal, it was their job to assist crews, day or night, in getting their craft through the locks as quickly and efficiently as possible, as well as recording passing traffic, collecting tolls (which would largely depend on the weight of the cargo) and taking mooring fees. On various systems today, there are a number of electro-hydraulic locks that are operated remotely from a control room and although these are

slowly being replaced by traditional types, there are still a few manned by permanent staff.

In addition to the traditional swing gate locks, there are also guillotine gates which lift vertically high enough above the level of the canal to give adequate headroom, sliding gates that retract sideways, and rotating gates which are curved to the arc they follow when opening or closing.

Operating a Lock

Each lock will be formed around a large stone or brick-lined chamber within which the level of the water can be raised or lowered. At each end of this chamber is a heavy wooden or steel gate, or two half 'mitre' gates that when closed from an 18 degree V-shape facing up-stream and, by the pressure of the water alone, forced together to create a watertight seal. This ingenious arrangement prevents one set of gates to be opened if the other set is not

locks, they will commonly consist of paddles (small sluice gates also known as cloughs) either plugging the ends of culverts tunnelled through the retaining stone walls around the sides of the main gates, or actually built into the main gates. Some locks have both types of paddle which greatly speeds up the job of filling or emptying the chamber. Mooring bollards are also a feature to help a boatman operate a lock, if and when necessary, single-handedly.

When a boatman wishes to descend from the upper canal level to the lower one, for example, there needs to be a sequence of events at each lock before he can continue his journey.

Depending on the last time the lock was used, the water in the chamber will be aligned with either the upper or lower pounds, and prior to opening the top or 'head' gate, it is necessary to check that the chamber is full, or if not, to open a paddle to fill it. Different authorities experimented with a variety of winding gear mechanisms to lift the paddles including worm and wheels or capstan and chains, but eventually the majority of operators settled upon rack-and-pinion. A cranked handle (or 'windlass) usually carried on the boat

closed properly. There are also two separate valve systems, one to let water into the chamber to fill it, the other to empty it, and these valves were made in various guises. On most British

is inserted into a cog (the 'pinion') engaging with a toothed bar (the 'rack') and by turning this handle, the paddle lifts and water from the upper level steadily fills the lock chamber. The rack is prevented from sliding back down by a small lever (or pawl) that engages with the pinion. Once this process is complete, the top gates can be opened by pushing hard on the long wooden balance beams that overhang the lock side, and the boat then enters the lock. Safely through, the top gate is moved back into the closed position and after ensuring the paddles are also securely shut, all attention turns to the bottom or 'tail' gate.

Now a second set of paddles need to be opened to slowly empty the lock chamber and bring the water (and of course the narrow boat) down to the level of the lower reaches before the tail gate can be pushed open, permitting the boat to leave the lock and continue onto the next leg of its journey.

If two or more boats are following one another, then the whole sequence described above is repeated for each. Once the last vessel has successfully negotiated the lock, the second gate from which it has exited is usually left

open for the convenience of a boat coming in the opposite direction.

And for boatmen wishing to ascend from the lower canal level to the upper level, the process is simply reversed.

Above: *Mitre type lock gates close at an angle of 18 degrees and are held together by the pressure of the water behind*

Above: *Electro-hydraulically operated lock gates at Fort Augustus on the Caledonian Canal*

As one can imagine, when businesses relied on the canal to transport raw material and bulk goods, the use of locks to gain or descend height would often prove to be a long and laborious process especially if the locks were grouped in relatively quick succession. The operating procedure for each lock would generally take anywhere between ten minutes for an experienced crew to twenty minutes for the novice but the task was not without its faults.

One of the biggest drawbacks with relying on several locks to descend a hill was that each time one was used, the volume of water minus the amount displaced by the boat was lost from the higher pound. If this pound had an inadequate water supply from a feeder spring, river, nearby lake or reservoir, then back-pumping systems needed to be introduced to maintain levels, drawing water from the lower reaches to replenish the upper sections. A pumping station located adjacent to a tightly packed flight of locks, however,

would make better economic sense than one attempting to siphon the same amount of water to an equivalent rise of individual locks spread over a greater distance.

Leaving the paddles of the head gate open whilst lifting those on the tail gate, could also mean water running freely from the upper pound to the lower levels. Preventing water loss of any kind was and still is the greatest concern to every canal authority.

Another predicament a crew could

find themselves in was that if a boat was positioned too close to either lock gate when the water was being emptied from the chamber, then the hull could catch or 'hang' on that gate or indeed the head sill – a curved man-made ledge between the base of the top gate and the floor of the lock. In such cases, as the water level continued to fall, there was the danger that the other end of the vessel might drop below the water line, swamping the interior and sinking the boat entirely. To hardened and

experienced commercial boatmen of the 1800s, this sort of naivety would have been inexcusable but with more and more holidaymakers and day trippers having since taken to Britain's waterways since the 1960s, this type of incident has unfortunately become an all too real occurrence, albeit still a relatively rare one.

To witness a lock in action, especially if there are several locks together, has always been of considerable fascination to those sightseers attracted to the canal side, and there are a great many examples of restored flights and staircases located around the British Isles.

Caen Hill

A 1715 Act of Parliament gave the go ahead for the Kennet & Avon to be built with a planned link from the River Thames at Reading to the River Avon at Bath, providing a continuous 86½ mile waterway cutting right across southern England. Taking eight years to complete, the canal left the easternmost point, Reading, and rose out of the Kennet Valley climbing over the Hampshire Downs and following the Vale of Pewsey. The 55 locks in this

section were, for the most part, fairly evenly spread with only the Crofton Flight (nine locks) and Wootton Rivers Flight (four locks) slowing progress on the construction.

To avoid huge loss of water from the highest levels to the lower reaches, a pumping house was built at Crofton, and the Boulton and Watt steam engine that was later installed in 1812 is today the oldest working beam engine in the world.

From the other end, the route headed east making use of the course of the River Avon through Hanham Mills to the centre of Bath from where the man-made section began. Following a fairly gentle path, the canal then made two crossings of the river via aqueducts, the first of these becoming probably the most celebrated architectural structure on the system. The three-arch Dundas Aqueduct, erected at Monkton Combe adjacent to the junction with the Somersetshire Coal Canal, was finished in Bath Stone

Above: *The canal basin at Bath on the River Avon with the city's famous Pultney Bridge in the background.*

Far Left: *A crane barge comes to the rescue of Ice Dragon after it had capsized and sunk in a lock*

Above: *Dundas Aqueduct on the Kennet & Avon*

to a John Rennie design that included some quite ostentatious features such as Doric pilasters and balustrades.

After leaving the River at Bradford-on-Avon, the canal then continued out across the Vale of Malmesbury and although this and the section from Reading were completed and ready to use by 1805 there was one obstacle still to overcome. On the western side of Devizes, Rennie and chief engineer, John Thomas, faced their biggest challenge – Caen Hill, a gradient of 1 in 44 that ascends 237 feet from the

Vale of Malmesbury up into the centre of the Wiltshire market town. Caen Hill was going to require some major excavation work.

From Lower Foxhangers Bridge to Devizes Town Bridge (sited next to what is now the Wadworth Brewery building), Rennie managed to squeeze in a total of twenty-nine locks, sixteen of these in a continuous and consecutive flight. Due to the terrain, there was little room for the conventional in-line water pounds between each set of gates and instead fifteen basins were dug out to the side.

Opened fully in 1810, Caen Hill is truly an extraordinary masterpiece of civil engineering. The earthworks undertaken in this two mile section has resulted in one of the most iconic and photographed sections on any of Britain's inland waterways.

Tardebigge Locks

Five years after Caen Hill commenced operation, another even more impressive flight opened 70 miles away on the Worcester & Birmingham Canal.

In 1791, a Bill was passed in Parliament giving permission for a canal to be built from a basin on Birmingham's Gas Street to Diglis in Worcester. There had been huge opposition to the scheme, mainly from management of the Birmingham Canal and of the Staffordshire & Worcestershire Canal who could foresee their respective systems losing business. This was especially worrying for the people of Stourport who had seen their town develop simply out of passing waterborne trade. Nevertheless, representatives from the Worcester & Birmingham argued that by aiming straight for Worcester, many boats could avoid the notorious Severn shallows further upstream and although they got their way, the Birmingham Canal Company made sure they had the last word. They pushed through another Act of Parliament stipulating that the Worcester and Birmingham could come no nearer to their system than 7 feet, preventing an actual link up! For an astonishing eight years, boats from Worcester that were transporting goods that needed taking on further were forced to stop and transfer their cargos across a 7-foot wide dock to a waiting vessel moored on the Birmingham Canal!

But before such farcical behaviour could take place, there was the small matter of building the Worcester & Birmingham in the first place with a route having been planned out by Josiah Clowes and John Snape. From Gas Street via Bourneville to King's Norton things went smoothly enough until the first major obstacle was encountered. Rather than going up and over the top, the engineers chose to dig a 2,726 yard tunnel through Wast Hill. Two more tunnels were required further on and whilst the excavation of Wast Hill had begun in 1794, it was not until 1807 that the next eight miles were fully ready for navigation! The massive delay had been caused by the need to build a number of small reservoirs and connecting streams to sustain water levels.

The third tunnel breached a hill above the village of Tardebigge, a few miles south of Bromsgrove. Installing reservoirs had severely taken its toll on the company purse strings and before anymore work could be done, the plans required a rethink to save money. The immediate dilemma facing the construction team was how to continue the canal from Tardebigge Wharf down a 2-mile gradient to the village

of Stoke Prior that sat on a level, 220 feet below. As the management team debated, the workforce was disbanded and over the following months nothing more was done.

In that time however, a fresh face, John Woodhouse, was appointed in the role of chief engineer and under his direction, a new scheme was implemented. He persuaded his managers that much of the descent could be accomplished via a series of hand-operated lifts and although his superiors were not entirely convinced, he was allowed to demonstrate his ideas with a single example constructed close to the Wharf. Counterbalanced with a weight made of bricks, it was designed so that two men would be capable, through an intricate series of chains and pulleys, of hoisting its wooden caisson of 64 tonnes from one level to the other. In practice the men employed on site could raise or lower more than one hundred boats per day but problems with the mechanism were soon encountered and after only four years of use, work had begun on its quite magnificent replacement.

Having secured more funding, the powers that be decided there was

Left: *The magnificent Caen Hill Flight of twenty nine consecutive locks*

nothing for it but to close the gap between Tardebigge Wharf and a point near Stoke Prior with one continuous flight consisting of no less than thirty locks! Together with Stoke Flight which comprises of six locks and is located immediately adjacent to the village, this 2-mile stretch of canal constituted the highest concentration of locks anywhere in the country. Work was completed in 1815 and within months of opening Tardebigge Flight, John Woodhouse's Lift had been consigned to the scrap heap.

The Leeds & Liverpool Canal – A Fantastic Feat of Engineering

Before the advent of the railway, one of the most ambitious waterways built in Britain and certainly the most important and prosperous trade route across the country was the Leeds & Liverpool Canal. The Aire & Calder Navigation had already linked Leeds city centre with the Yorkshire coal fields to the east, the inland ports of Wakefield and Castleford, and the Humber Estuary beyond. The construction of the Leeds & Liverpool would not only reward the collieries of Lancashire with a profitable market on Merseyside, but also provide lucrative business opportunities for the Lancashire textile industry as well as helping to forge a waterway east to west from the North Sea at Hull to the Irish Sea at Liverpool.

From the Aire & Calder Navigation, the new canal left Leeds and meandered west, parallel with the River Aire to Keighley, before heading out towards Skipton high up in the southern reaches of the magnificent North Yorkshire Moors. At Gargrave, it zigzagged south, through the great sprawl of fulling mills in Burnley, Accrington and the city of Blackburn where the manufacturing of fabric during the Georgian period was profoundly responsible for shaping the local economy. By the end of the 19th Century Burnley, for example, was the world's leading producer of cotton cloth. The fact that there were also huge seams of coal beneath the

Above: *Leeds and Liverpool Canal*

surface could only be beneficial to local businesses, the new waterway would provide long-term employment for the working population.

From Blackburn the canal tortuously corkscrewed its way into Liverpool Docks passing through Chorley, Wigan, Burscough Bridge and Maghull, with various arms branching off to Rufford and the navigable River Douglas, from Wigan through Leigh and the connection with the Bridgewater Canal, to Walton Summit just south of Preston, and to Bradford (via Shipley) – a vital link for that city's industries.

Preceded by the Huddersfield Narrow and the Rochdale systems, the Leeds & Liverpool was the third man-

made waterway to traverse the Pennines.

The idea to attempt such a formidable project had first been mooted in 1766 and surveying the 127-mile route was placed in the hands of John Longbotham whilst renowned canal engineer, James Brindley was called in to adjust certain aspects and sections to tap into the most affluent industrial districts.

Excavation began in 1770 and within seven years, two quite different stretches were open for business. At the western end, a level 27 miles had been completed from Liverpool to Newburgh without the need for a single lock installation outside of the city. At the eastern end, however, 33 miles from Leeds to Gargrave included thirty locks, twenty-three of which climbing through eight staircases! At 487 feet above sea level, Skipton was the highest point the canal would reach and in the town of Bingley, halfway between Shipley and Keighley, two separate staircases in close proximity saw the canal gain a height of 90 feet. One of these, Bingley Five-Rise, comprised of four chambers and five gates allowing boats to rise more than 59 feet over a distance measuring just 320 feet and, with a gradient of 1 in 5, remains the steepest lock staircase in Britain. Waiting in the lower basin to use Bingley Five-Rise with the gates looming ominously up ahead could undoubtedly be a daunting experience!

After 31 miles, the western section had reached Appley Bridge and the start of the ascent towards Wigan. Here the first locks since leaving Liverpool were needed to effect the climb. But, as the saying goes, 'you wait all day for a bus to come and then three come along at once', at Wigan the 3-mile gradient past the ironworks and blast furnaces of New Springs required no less than twenty-one consecutive locks to overcome the 180 foot rise. This amounted to the third highest number of locks in one flight in Britain after Caen Hill and Tardebigge.

In 1781, the money ran out, construction ground to a halt and the nation's attention turned to war in America. It would be another ten years before things started moving again and this time under the supervision of a new Chief Engineer, Robert Whitworth.

In 1791 there were over 45 miles separating the two sections of the Leeds & Liverpool with Whitworth's biggest challenges still lying ahead. As progress on the eastern end slowly made its way

Far Left: *Leeds and Liverpool Canal at Skipton*

from Gargrave towards Barrowford, he resubmitted plans for the next stage through Burnley. This latest scheme included boring new tunnels at Foulridge and Gannow, and construction of a north-south embankment dissecting Burnley completely. The town straddled the Calder Valley and rather than utilise locks on either slope, Whitworth calculated that keeping the canal on a level plane would be a much better option even if it did require some stupendously major earthworks.

It took six years before Foulridge tunnel was fit for use and whilst it was being dug, a temporary wharf at the northern portal provided a transhipment point for vessels from the River Humber and Aire & Calder Navigation carrying cotton imported from America.

Beyond the southern end of the tunnel, another flight of locks were built at Barrowford so the canal could descend to a level that would take it the last 5 miles through Burnley's suburbs on its approach to the town centre.

Foulridge tunnel hit the headlines in 1912 with an incident involving a cow named 'Buttercup' (well it had to be called that really didn't it!?!). After falling in the water and having attempted to find an alternative way out, the poor unfortunate beast resorted to swimming the entire 1,640 yards of tunnel in complete darkness only to be rescued at the other end suffering from exhaustion. According to local legend, she was only revived when a group of drinkers who had wandered over from a nearby pub (appropriately named 'The Hole in the Wall') administered her with a good dose of alcohol!

On the southern side of Calder Valley, the 559 yard Gannow Tunnel was started and to bridge the gap between this and the town, work also began on the Burnley Embankment. Taking 5 years to complete, the 'Straight Mile' as it was nicknamed (even though it was closer to ¾ mile long) measured 60 feet tall, towered high above the factory rooftops, and featured a short aqueduct over the River Calder.

During World War II, it was drained several times when government officials feared this colossal landmark would become an easy target for the Luftwaffe. The Embankment contained such a huge volume of water that a breach in the sides would almost certainly have flooded the town with catastrophic results.

By the turn of the Century, the canal's construction had got as far as Clayton-Le-Moors and although this section did not involve any major engineering work beyond the norm, the navvies were once again forced to down tools as funding dried up. And yet again it was due to another war, this time with Napoleon, that investors were becoming increasingly reluctant to part with their money. The converging ends of the two sections, east and west, were now tantalisingly close with only the section from Blackburn to Wigan needed to bridge the gap.

Before becoming chief engineer for the Leeds & Liverpool, Robert Whitworth had been employed as

a surveyor for a new venture, the Lancaster Canal. It was his job to determine the most appropriate route linking Westhoughton, a mining community 5 miles east of Wigan with the town of Kendal, 60 miles north on the eastern fringes of the Lake District. The path that Whitworth proposed would not only cut through Preston, Lancaster and Carnforth but for a short distance run parallel to the Leeds & Liverpool before crossing over near

Chorley. By signing an agreement with Lancaster Canal's management committee, he was able to adjust each course slightly so that both canal companies could share an amalgamated section between two junctions, one west of Wigan and the other at Johnson's Hill just north of Chorley. Whilst the Lancaster Canal Company's team of navvies pressed on with their northern section from Preston to Kendal, they entrusted the southern end

Above: *Burnley Embankment carries the Leeds & Liverpool Canal 60 feet above the roofs of the town*

to Whitworth's men. At the Johnson's Hill junction, a 3½–mile arm was also constructed in the direction of Preston and for the time being this masqueraded as the Walton Summit Branch of the Leeds & Liverpool until a time when the northern and southern ends of the Lancaster system could be joined. Plans to build an aqueduct to cross the Ribble were, however, shelved on the grounds of cost and there the southern end of the Lancaster Canal remained never to be extended nor, unfortunately, to ever reach Westhoughton.

The Leeds & Liverpool, however, was finally completed in 1816 and remained in regular commercial operation for over 150 years, long after World War II. Coal and textiles made up the lion's share of cargo carried

and the broad locks of 14-foot wide of which there were more than ninety, allowed uncommonly large-capacity vessels and barges (up to a maximum length of 62 feet) to navigate over its entire 128 miles.

When two particularly cold spells froze much of the main channel during the 1960s, the canal lost any remaining trade to other transport systems unaffected by the extreme wintry conditions. But unlike the other two trans-Pennines routes, the Leeds & Liverpool never actually closed and was able to quickly adapt and cater for the up-and-coming leisure industry. It would be more than thirty years before the Huddersfield Narrow and the Rochdale were restored and could tap into the same market.

Lifts, Planes & the Wheel

Far Right:

Anderton Boat Lift was built in 1875 to link the Trent & Mersey to the Weaver Navigation. Note a barge being lowered in the right-hand caisson

Anderton Boat Lift

In 1777, the 93 mile Trent & Mersey was opened, allowing vessels from Shardlow on the outskirts of Nottingham to travel south-west to Burton-on-Trent before turning north through Stoke-on-Trent, Kidsgrove, Middlewich and Northwich. One of its main proponents was Josiah Wedgwood who recognised that the canal with its smooth, calm and unchanging conditions was the most appropriate way to transport his pottery. Roads at that time were unpaved, rutted and often flooded to the point of being impassable and were therefore quite unsuitable for the carriage of fragile crockery. Wedgwood not only gained access to greater markets via Merseyside but with the Trent & Mersey linking into the Bridgewater Canal at Preston Brook, he could also tap into customers in areas served by other adjoining canal networks.

During the late-19th Century, and under the directorship of Edward Leader Williams, a twenty mile navigable stretch of the broad River Weaver was developed between Winsford and Runcorn. Barges would travel north to unload their cargos onto larger sea-going vessels at the bustling docks of Liverpool – the salt they carried being a valuable commodity used to preserve food in the days before refrigeration. Unfortunately, the salt companies found that the Weaver Navigation somewhat

hampered their trade routes by the fact that the river was 50 feet below the level of the Trent & Mersey Canal. If they were to market the salt to a wider area, the precious goods had to be transferred from one vessel to another at Northwich where both waterways came into close proximity – a time consuming and far from ideal state of affairs.

Williams set about finding someone who could come up with a solution to this problem and finally settled upon Edwin Clark, a contemporary of the great Robert Stephenson. Clark had been employed as the Superintending Engineer on Stephenson's magnificent Menai Bridge project and the designs he presented to Williams resulted in the construction of the Anderton Boat Lift – a wonderful testament to the golden age of British engineering.

Whilst working on the Menai Bridge, Clark developed an expertise for hydraulic devices as they were used to hoist the bridge's main tubular components into place.

The Anderton Boat Lift featured a pair of enormous water containers or caissons set next to one another within a vast iron framework and, on the upper

level, a 165-foot long feeder aqueduct. It worked on the basis that as one caisson descended, so it would counterbalance with the ascending one, elevated or lowered by hydraulic rams.

Each ram was 3 feet in diameter encased within a shaft sunk 56 feet into the ground below the river bed. A single caisson weighed 91 tonnes empty and 252 tonnes when full of water and measured 75 feet long by 50 feet wide. When fully loaded, four narrow boats could be moved at any one time, two in each caisson, a factor that greatly sped up the process of transferring

goods from the Weaver Navigation to the Trent & Mersey and vice-versa. It was the first of its kind anywhere in the world and must have been quite a draw for sightseers during those innocent times when one had to make his or her own entertainment.

The Lift in its original form functioned almost continuously for nearly thirty years before a major overhaul was required. In 1904 work began to modify this famous landmark with an extra deck mounted high above the top level. On to this was installed new machinery consisting of 72 pulley wheels – 16

Above: *A sightseeing barge entering the Lift from the Trent & Mersey through the guillotine type gates*

large wheels attached to both lifting and safety cables, 20 wheels each bearing two lifting cables, and 36 each with one cable – and an apportioned number of 7 tonne counterweights. The additional equipment proved to be of great success and, in 1908, the Lift recommenced its important role as the link between the two waterways. For the next 75 years, it performed admirably and would not cease working again until the mid-1980s when some of the structure was discovered to be suffering from serious corrosion. At the time, the costs would have been too high to put things right so the Lift was closed.

Salvation came in 2000 when restoration began, financed in no small part by a £3.3 million grant secured through the Heritage Lottery Fund. For two years, the work continued which included replicating the original hydraulic rams thus returning to the old form of operation, whilst preserving the top-deck pulley wheels and associated machinery for posterity. All the efforts of British Waterways came to fruition in March 2002 when the Anderton Boat

Lift once again embarked on a new lease of life serving the leisure craft and tourist industry.

Foxton Inclined Plane

At the beginning of the 1800s, construction began on a 24½ mile link between the Leicestershire & Northants Union and the Grand Junction canals which together would create a direct and unquestionably profitable route from the coalfields around Nottingham to the great factories of London. Opened in 1814, the Grand Union as it was called, (and not to be confused with the current much larger system of the same name), followed a constant level for much of its length and only when reaching Foxton was any major engineering work required. Situated some three miles west of Market Harborough, the terrain here dropped 75 feet and to overcome the descent, engineers for the Grand Union put in place a flight of ten locks. These were built as a set of two staircases but as with so many other staircases around the country, the drawback to this type of system, and especially at Foxton, was that thousands of gallons of water were used

with the passing of each narrow boat and in times of water shortages, operation occasionally had to be suspended.

Each lock was built to the canal standard width of 7 feet allowing only

Above: Foxton Locks link the Leicestershire & Northants Union to the Grand Junction

one boat at a time into each lock. Vessels could be forced to queue for hours until being called forward, either to descend through the flight to the lowest level or vice-versa. Negotiating the flight would take around 45 minutes (or around 55 minutes for a pair of boats) in either direction. In the sleepy days before railways spread far and wide across the land, this delay seemed of little importance and operations continued unabated for almost the next century. When large businesses began to send freight by rail, however, the canal's future came under serious threat and a new system needed introducing at Foxton to speed things up.

One idea was to make every lock bigger to accommodate vessels two at a time, but this was swiftly rejected as it would have increased water usage astronomically. Instead, Gordon Cale Thomas, chief engineer of the Grand Junction Canal Company came up with an ambitious solution. He designed a lift consisting of two water filled caissons travelling up and down an inclined plane on steel rails. Each container weighed a constant 230 tons with a combined space in the two caissons for four vessels. They were attached together by a cable wound round a drum at the top of the plane and as one ascended to the top level it would be counterbalanced by the other descending until the latter touched the surface of the water. At this point, its buoyancy would offset the weight of the ascending caisson. To compensate for this effect, Thomas ingeniously built the upper reaches of the incline to a lesser gradient thus easing the load not only on the cable but the stationary steam engine powering the drum.

A capacity of four boats could be transferred in one go, taking just 12 minutes to complete the operation. Therefore at the busiest of times, using the Lift proved almost ten times quicker than the flight of locks, yet with comparatively no loss of water.

For a very short period Foxton Incline Plane was deemed a success but as transporting goods by canal gradually fell out of favour, the cost of maintaining and staffing this rather Heath-Robinson but nevertheless wonderful creation was too much of a financial burden for the Grand Junction Canal Company. By 1911 the Lift operation had been suspended and less than thirty years after it opened, Gordon Cale Thomas' engineering masterpiece had been bought

by the scrap man. With all the major mechanical components dismantled and removed off site, the story of this marvel of engineering could have ended there and then. Today, however, there are those campaigning to recreate the Lift in all its former glory as a working monument to its Victorian creator.

Falkirk Wheel

Possibly the most ambitious modern day feat of British waterways engineering has been the construction of the Millennium Link between the Forth & Clyde Canal and the Union Canal.

When originally completed, the Forth & Clyde stretched from Clydebank west of Glasgow, right across to Grangemouth on the banks of the Forth whilst the Union, a waterway that broadly ran a few miles south but parallel to the Forth, served Edinburgh city centre at its eastern-most terminus. The Union was opened in 1822 and was built mainly for the carriage of coal from collieries positioned along its route to the Scottish capital. For almost its entire length, its course followed a constant altitude, 240 feet above sea level. Both systems converged two miles west of Falkirk and in order to reach the basin in Camelon

115 feet below, boats travelling from the Union had to descend through a flight of eleven locks. As more freight was taken by road or rail, however, the importance of these canals diminished and eventually the connecting locks were lost entirely in the early-1930s when the pounds and chambers were filled in.

As holidaying by boat grew in popularity, thoughts once again turned to how the isolated Union could be reunited with its neighbouring waterway but it was not until 1994 that plans for the Falkirk Wheel were first mooted.

Residential and commercial buildings now covered the area where once the flight of eleven locks had originally graced the landscape and a new site, less than a mile west, was identified as the best location to begin the new construction.

The designs drawn up at the Nicoll Russell Studios in Dundee featured two beautifully sculpted armatures attached to a central spindle, each bearing a large caisson of a combined weight of 600 tonnes.

Similar to a Ferris wheel at the fair, as the whole rotational part of the

structure turned, so the caissons would be maintained in an upright position, but just to be sure, each one would also operate off a series of toothed gears.

For sheer convenience, it might be thought that all components would have been made in Scotland, but this was not the case and were in fact fabricated at the Butterley Engineering Steelworks, some 250 miles south in Derbyshire. These were then transported in sections by lorry north of the border in 2001. A year later, the Falkirk Wheel was complete and opened in May by Her Majesty The Queen.

From the old route that once linked up with the previous flight of locks, the canal today continues several hundred yards west before turning sharp to the north and entering the new Rough Castle Tunnel. Having negotiated 365 yards of darkness, each boat will then emerge into daylight and within a basin just prior to crossing onto a concrete and steel aqueduct directly before the Wheel. Although all interest is usually focussed on Wheel, the aqueduct that carries the Union on the approach to the rotating

armatures is itself a remarkable piece of architecture. With the bridge piers echoing the curved lines of the wheel, a tunnel of five steel loops creates an almost ceremonial archway – their reflection in the water completing each circle.

At this point the canal stretches ahead towards the horizon and seems to end abruptly and disconcertingly in mid-air. Once entered into the top-most caisson, a steel gate seals the water and boat within the container. The Wheel can operate equally as efficiently whether there is one caisson occupied or if both contain vessels as the weight of each boat, however large or small, displaces an equal mass of water meaning that the caissons will always support the exact same load. And because they are positioned directly opposite on either side of the rotating spindle, each caisson counterbalances the other as the Wheel turns.

Not only does the Falkirk Wheel solve the problem of transferring canal boats 115 feet down from the Union to the Forth & Clyde, but it has become the area's most popular tourist attraction and for a nominal fee, many visitors will pay just to take a trip from the upper to the lower level!

Bridging the Gap

Whilst locks, lifts, and inclined planes were all very well when overcoming isolated gradients, they were much too costly when making a relatively short crossing between two areas of high ground. The cheapest alternative when traversing a valley or depression would often be to build an aqueduct.

The concept was by no means a British invention of the Georgian era as in pre-Christian times, numerous Roman and Greek aqueducts were introduced running at ground level, on embankments or through tunnels, to sustain water in rural areas for farming or urban districts for sanitary purposes. The Romans became especially adept at digging irrigation ditches, channels for conveying water to their great cities, and eventually networks of transport canals.

The earliest record of an aqueduct in use, however, was from as far back as 691 BC when a single span structure linked two sides of a valley at Jerwan in Assyria, or modern day Iraq. Built by slave labour in the reign of Sennacherib, it not only brought vital water supplies to the city of Nineveh but kept the moat that surrounded the vast city walls topped up.

When man-made waterways were exploited as transport arteries in the 1600s most aqueducts in this country followed a tried and tested practice of using stone as the material of choice. But in the 18th Century, foundries had

become the cornerstone of Britain's Industrial Revolution and during the golden age of canal development, literally hundreds of aqueducts were constructed comprising of immense U-shaped iron troughs located across stone or brick piers. With 4,000 miles of navigable inland waterways still in existence, many of these quite extraordinary landmarks have survived with the majority having undergone complete restoration to original condition.

Pontcysyllte Aqueduct

One of the largest structures ever to grace British waterways and one

Right: *Ellesmere Canal Basin*

of the most popular tourist attractions in Wales today is the magnificent and awe-inspiring Pontcysyllte Aqueduct. It was designed by Thomas Telford and built to traverse the River Dee between the villages of Froncysyllte and Trefor.

In 1793, an Act of Parliamentary granted permission for the Ellesmere Canal to be built from the Mersey to the Severn. Gaining profitable trade along the route via Chester, Wrexham, Ruabon and Shrewsbury its potential cargo would include coal, iron and limestone. Another Act that same year saw a separate organisation, the Montgomery Canal Company, begin excavation from Newtown in Powys to link up to one of the Ellesmere's branches at Llanymynech by following parallel to the Severn through Welshpool.

Within three years the Ellesmere Canal was earning its keep with a completed section between Chester (where a junction was made with the Chester Canal – Chester to Middlewich), and a new Merseyside harbour at Netherpool. As it was eventually going to tap into the rich Shropshire coal seams around Ellesmere (from where the canal's name originated), Netherpool's identity was changed to Ellesmere Port to reflect the intended connection.

With 18th Century roads as bad as they were, it was quicker to get from Chester into Liverpool by boat than it was by road, and a passenger service commenced almost immediately to help fund the canal build. But instead of continuing south from Chester, construction moved twenty miles inland with all attention turning to utilising the River Dee close to Berwyn for a continuous water supply for the rest of the system, as well as a second connection with the Chester Canal east at Hurleston Junction near Nantwich. It was at this point that the managing committee commissioned Telford to build his magnificent aqueduct as the deep river valley had to be bridged.

His plans consisted of nineteen hollow stone piers each set over 52 feet apart, with the water being carried high above the ground in a 1,007 foot long trough constructed from enormous cast iron plates bolted together and made watertight using Welsh flannel, white lead and iron particles locally sourced from Ruabon. The trough would not, however, be physically attached to any part of the supporting stone or iron superstructure and instead would only rest in place. Along one side of the trough, Telford provided a towpath with a safely guard rail whereas on the other side, it was a case of hold on tight and don't look down! With only a token 12 inches of iron parapet above the water line to prevent any canal slopping over the edge and plunging 126 feet into the valley below, a helmsman who could confidently take his barge across the aqueduct would have had to have had a good head for heights!

In November 1805, the aqueduct was officially opened and the canal reached as far as Trefor. From there, it turned sharply to the west continuing just beyond Llangollen to Llantysilio, close to Berwyn, to a weir on the Dee known as Horseshoe Falls. This section would take a further three years to complete before fresh water from the Clwydian and Berwyn Range was flowing into the southern part of Ellesmere Canal. Many years later, this vital source would prove essential in keeping the canal from falling into disrepair in a time when other waterways built for commercial use had become redundant,

overgrown, and silted up.

As for the rest of Ellesmere Canal, the dream to link Trefor north to Chester via Ruabon and Wrexham never materialised and the two parts remained connected only via the Chester Canal. There were several branches, one into the centre of Whitchurch, one to Quina Brook (although this was a somewhat half-

the limestone quarries of Llanymynech where the Ellesmere joined into the Montgomery Canal meandering up alongside the Severn from Garthmyl, some 5½ miles south of Welshpool. Eventually the Montgomery would reach its intended destination at Newtown but that would not be until 1821, thirty years after this waterway was started.

The Ellesmere and Chester Canals were amalgamated in 1813 before joining forces with the Birmingham & Liverpool Junction Canal in an attempt to stave off competition from the railways. In 1845, the two systems became one with the emergence of the Shropshire Union Railways & Canal Company and from then on, the section consisting of Pontcysyllte Aqueduct and the extension to the Dee became known as the Llangollen Branch of the Shropshire Union Canal. In 2009, it received the honourable title of World Heritage Site in that years UNESCO listings.

hearted attempt to make for the clay pits of Prees but never quite got there), and a short stub into the market town of Ellesmere. Of most importance was a branch south from Lower Frankton to

Barton Swing Aqueduct

Sir Edward Leader Williams, who had previously worked on

the Anderton Boat Lift project in the late 1800s, had since become Chief Engineer and architect of the Manchester Ship Canal.

During that same period, the Bridgewater Canal and all its holdings had come under the custodianship of the Ship Canal Company who set about making some improvements to their newly-acquired subsidiary. James Brindley's original stone aqueduct at Barton–upon–Irwell had stood in place since 1761 when that section of the Bridgewater was opened to link Worsley Delph with Stretford. Its height above the River Irwell was of little importance in those days but when the Ship Canal was built, it made use of the conveniently placed river as a route into the city and the restricted clearance under the aqueduct was wholly inadequate for modern vessels. Sadly, the aging structure once described as 'one of the seven wonders of the canal age', had to go.

Although the use of a flight of locks at this point was considered, the idea was quickly discarded as the degree of engineering involved plus the continual loss of water during use would never have proved cost effective. Instead,

Williams put pen to paper and designed a magnificent yet monstrous swing bridge that could turn through 90 degrees out of the way of passing traffic whilst still retaining the canal level of the old aqueduct.

The first part of the scheme required the building of an island alongside the Ship Canal upon which a stone base would be laid demarcating the new aqueduct's pivot point. The upper waterway would span the gap via a giant 235 foot long trough with gates at each end to contain the 800 tonnes of water whilst it was rotating. Needless to say two further sluice type gates would also be required at the corresponding ends of the canal to prevent those pounds emptying.

The Derbyshire foundry of Andrew Handyside were tasked with fabricating and installing the 650 tonne iron trough and on the 21st August 1893, a boat containing dignitaries, invited guests and members of management from both canal companies made the first crossing.

After more than a hundred years, Barton Swing Aqueduct is still in operation and this Grade II Listed Building is regarded as one of the jewels of Britain's canal network.

Left: *A famous landmark on the Shropshire Union Canal is High Bridge. Note the telegraph pole in its own archway*

Going Underground

The surveyors and architects tasked with planning many of Britain's systems understood the benefits of using contour lines when crossing difficult terrain. In upland areas, canals would occupy shelves cut into the hillsides in an attempt to reduce the number of ascents and descents, therefore making huge savings on expenditure and labour, but above all helping to sustain water supply. Where necessary, however, the work might occasionally involve some of the most ambitious and challenging ventures in civil engineering. In the majority of cases, single or indeed flights of locks would be introduced to overcome particularly steep gradients so that working boats plying their trade between the great industrial towns and cities could continue their journeys unabated. Sometimes, however, routing a canal up and over the vast and bleak tracts of high ground that stood in a builder's path would prove much too costly and, instead, it was deemed more economical to burrow straight through the ground.

The ultimate aim was to connect sources of raw material and foodstuffs with factories, commercial centres and potential markets, and many important canal links were only realised with the completion of some extraordinarily long tunnels. In the late-1700s, these would not only have been considered vital for the transport of essential goods

and commodities but also celebrated as wonderful achievements, especially as most tunnels would have been dug almost entirely by hand once particularly tough seams in the rock strata had been blasted with dynamite.

Whilst a heavy horse was quite content and capable of pulling loaded boats along canal towpaths out in the open, it was quite a different matter once entering a tunnel and some horses were ill at ease in the dark dank confines. In many cases it was far easier and safer to walk the animals over the hill to the other tunnel portal whilst the boatmen 'legged' their vessels through – a technique by which the crew lay on their backs and pushed with their feet along the tunnel ceiling. To save precious time, steam, diesel and even electric tugs were later employed just to perform this specific task.

Norwood Tunnel

The first canal tunnel to measure over a mile in length was bored through

Above: *Sapperton Tunnel*

a limestone ridge south-east of Sheffield. Norwood Tunnel was the final section of the Chesterfield Canal, connecting Chesterfield itself to the River Trent just north of Gainsborough. It was yet another brainchild of James Brindley, one of the greatest canal engineers of the 18th Century.

Once access shafts had been driven vertically down from the surface at regular intervals, teams were employed to continue laterally on both sides towards the next teams digging in the opposite direction. Prior to any work being undertaken, however, the surface had to be carefully surveyed to ensure that each shaft was excavated to its own individually calculated depth to maintain the same canal level along the entire route, whatever the rock type.

When it was finished in 1775, Norwood Tunnel was in fact more than 1½ miles long but within two years even that record would be surpassed – albeit by just 18½ yards – when Harecastle Tunnel opened on the Trent & Mersey.

Sapperton Tunnel

Between 1789 and 1811, Sapperton on the Thames & Severn Canal held the honour of being the longest

Above:
Standedge Tunnel at Marsden

tunnel in England. Taking five years to build, it punched a hole almost 2¼ miles in length through the Cotswold Hills between Stroud and Cirencester, but unlike other canal tunnels which are usually bored to a standard narrow boat width of just over 7 feet plus a towpath, Sapperton had to be wide enough not only to accommodate Thames barges of 12-foot beam, but also the 15 foot 'trows' that traditionally plied their trade along the River Severn. This of course pushed the cost of construction up considerably and, so as not to add to the rising expenditure, space for a towpath was deleted from the plans.

For the next twenty years, there were a number of tunnels excavated on various systems around the country that all exceeded a mile in length, and although Lapal on the Dudley No.2 Canal measured well over two miles, it fell 22 yards short of claiming Sapperton's crown.

Standedge Tunnel

In July 1795, contractor John Evans began work on Standedge Tunnel, its excavation following virtually a straight line between Diggle and Marsden. This would allow the Huddersfield Narrow Canal (also known as Sir John Ramsden's Canal) that had been in the making since the late 1770s, to pass through the southern reaches of the Pennines from Ashton-under-Lyne in Greater Manchester. Eventually it would connect up with the Calder & Hebble Navigation and waterways meandering their way through West Yorkshire.

Under the supervision of engineer Benjamin Outram and chief surveyor Nicholas Brown, digging started simultaneously from both ends where stationary steam engines were employed in an attempt to pump flood water out of the construction sites. Unfortunately, progress was hampered by a greater

water filtration than originally anticipated. With escalating costs, the managing committee had trouble paying the contractors and as the new century dawned, work ground to a halt. Within a year, Outram had resigned his position as Engineer although the build continued only sporadically and on a much tighter budget.

The situation improved in 1807 when the great Thomas Telford was asked to advise. His engineering expertise proved invaluable and in two years the ends of the tunnel had met, another two years and Standedge Tunnel was deemed complete and ready for use, and on the 4th April 1811, some sixteen years after the cutting of the first sod, a party of dignitaries made what should have been the first official sub-Pennine journey by boat. Unfortunately the previous delays meant that the Rochdale Canal had already made that claim seven years earlier.

At a staggering 5,698 yards or 3¼ miles in length, Standedge Tunnel holds the title of not only the longest canal tunnel in Britain, but also highest above sea level (643 feet) and deepest beneath the ground (636 feet below the surface between the highlands of Moss Moor and Wessenden Moor).

As with Sapperton Tunnel, build costs were kept to the absolute minimum and no tow-path was included so, once again, whilst the poor old horse took a well-earned rest, the poor old crew were required to 'leg' their boats the entire 3¼ miles!

Wider stretches were hollowed out at various stages along the route so that boats could pass oncoming traffic, but in practice this was rarely going to happen, probably because the boatmen wanted to spend as little time as possible in those dark, dank and undoubtedly rat infested conditions. As a result, large iron gates were positioned at each end to ensure that between certain times, boats could only travel in one or the other direction. As soon as the last of a string of waiting boats had entered the tunnel, an employee permanently based on site would lock the gate so effectively blocking that portal. Whilst those crews legged their way through, he would then guide the tow horses over the hill to meet up with the boats again on the other side where that gate would be unlocked to let the boats back out into daylight again. Once the tunnel was clear, he would indicate to more waiting craft that it

was their turn to enter the tunnel in the opposite direction, and this somewhat archaic procedure was maintained on a daily basis for over twenty years.

When transporting goods by canal fell out of favour, maintenance to tunnels went by the wayside and many became unstable and dangerous to travel through. Standedge Tunnel was used commercially for over 110 years but was declared unsafe soon after World War II, with the gates locked for what seemed like the last time around 1949.

The enthusiasm and desire to preserve all things of antiquity is part and parcel of the British psyche and in 2001, 190 years after Standedge first opened Britain's longest navigable underground waterway was once again restored to its former glory.

Although Sapperton Tunnel in Gloucestershire remains closed, there are plans in place to make it safe again and restore it for future generations to enjoy.

Strood Tunnel

One tunnel that will never again form part of the British canal system is Strood. When it was

Above:
Standedge Tunnel

completed, the Thames & Medway Canal was only 6½ miles long yet held the curious distinction of having over a third of its length rooted in permanent darkness. Opened in 1824 to join the River Thames at Gravesend with the River Medway at Rochester, 2¼ miles of the route incorporated Strood Tunnel, at one time the second longest canal tunnel in Britain. Driven in a perfect straight line through the chalk promontory called North Foreland, it was also the largest ever excavated with a bore over 35 feet high by 26 feet wide

Above: *Strood Tunnel in working days*

including towpath, affording enough room to accommodate the biggest Thames sailing barges with their masts folded down. This journey would cut the previous distance between the docks of Tilbury and Chatham by over twenty miles.

The rock strata would frequently cause problems for owners, the Thames & Medway Canal Company, however, and use of the tunnel was largely dependant on the state of the tides in the two rivers. Congestion regularly occurred at either end whilst boats wanting to use the route waited their turn. After only six years, a wide basin was excavated 1,530 yards in from the north end where the thickness of rock between the tunnel ceiling and the surface was at its least. To achieve this, a large hole was sunk down from

ground level dividing the one tunnel into two and immediately ending Strood's title as the second longest single canal tunnel in Britain.

After only 22 years of use as a commercial carrier, the tunnel was bought by the South Eastern Railway. The new owners wasted no time and filled the waterway in to the level of the towpath, and laid two railway tracks on top to create a more direct rail link into Central London from Canterbury.

Above: *There is little evidence today that Strood Tunnel was once plied by Thames Barges*

Restoration & Revival

Far Right: *This transhipment shed at Whaley Bridge was used to transfer goods from the Peak Forest Canal to the Cromford & High Peak Railway*

Since the 1960s, there have been numerous charity groups set up specifically to restore and revive abandoned and derelict canals. Without the sterling efforts of these volunteers offering their services and giving up their holiday time, hundreds of miles could not have been reopened. Because of the enthusiasm of such individuals, there is now a network of more than 4,000 miles spread across the country with that figure only set to rise with the completion of other ongoing projects.

Restoring a canal can cost millions of pounds but in addition, effective fund-raising has also allowed huge features engineered in the Georgian and Victorian periods to be renovated, not just cosmetically or as museum pieces, but put back into full working order to perform on a daily basis the tasks to which they were originally intended. Flights and staircases of locks, boat lifts, aqueducts and tunnels have all received attention so that vital connections between different sections of canal can be reopened and maintained.

As with the men who designed and built the canals in the 18th Century, there are many new obstacles to overcome. Members of the Manchester & Stockport Canal Society, for example, are having to figure out a way of reinstating certain sections that have collapsed through mining subsidence.

After the war, there were many

parts of cities especially around canal basins and warehouses that were left to deteriorate, and it is only in recent times that there have been council led schemes to rejuvenate these run down districts with new shopping outlets, cafes and walkways. These redevelopments can transform areas from dilapidated squalor into chic centres of commerce that are not only popular with day trippers and shoppers but often provide desirable premises for retailers and residents alike.

Some might think that, today, canals are only relics from our past industrial heritage, and whilst it is true that the majority of work focuses on bringing back to life existing sections, there are occasionally quite extraordinary schemes, even in this day and age, that aim to propose fresh and exciting ideas in order to extend and enhance Britain's waterway network.

Liverpool Canal Link

In 1846, the Leeds & Liverpool Canal finally gained direct access to the docks on Merseyside albeit thirty years after the canal had reached the city. Vessels could navigate from the North to the South docks before unloading cargos brought across from the North East or loading goods to take in the other direction.

When in the early part of the 20th Century the Docklands became the subject of a redevelopment scheme, Georges Dock was filled in to provide reclaimed land so that the Liver Building, Cunard Building and the Mersey Docks & Harbour Board

Building, more popularly known as the Three Graces, could be built in its place. This severed the link to the South docks and thereafter boats were required to take to the busy channels of the Mersey in order to get there.

As part of a program of regeneration along the river side, a new proposal was put forward in 2000 to reconnect the Leeds & Liverpool with Canning Dock taking a new route via Salisbury Dock, Princes Half Tide Dock, West Waterloo Dock, Princess Dock, past the new cruise liner terminus and across

Pier Head adding an extra 1½ miles on to the entire length of the Leeds & Liverpool.

The cost of building this new link came to £22 million and after three years in the making, was open on the 25th March 2009.

Bedford Link

During the early 1800s, brewer Samuel Whitbread expressed his intensions to build a broad watercourse linking the navigable reaches of the

Great Ouse to the Grand Union Canal, stretching some twenty miles between Bedford to a point close to what is now Milton Keynes. It was not until almost 200 years later, however, that there was enough support for the proposal to get the go-ahead from government and local authorities and that construction could finally begin.

Today we live in an age where jobs are becoming harder to come by, people are spending less, and more holidaymakers are choosing to take their vacations on home soil. It is hoped that the Bedford Link project will generate employment for nearly 1,000 people as well as attract many more visitors – an estimated 750,000 per annum – into the area.

The planned route will form a series of water parks that follow a course through Kempston and bypassing Cranfield, before joining the Grand Union east of Milton Keynes and will possibly feature a new concept in lock technology – the diagonal lock. The plan is for a giant reinforced concrete tube to be laid longitudinally at an angle down a slope with, at the top, a set of gates separating it from the upper navigable pound and, at the bottom, another set of doors that will form a watertight seal. When the tube is full, then boats will be able to enter through the open gates at the top. Once these are closed again, a valve at the base will empty the tube and the boat will descend inside surrounded by pontoons

to prevent it from scraping the sides.

Conversely, once the level of water is equal to that of the lower pound, a boat can enter through the open watertight doors and after the seal has been restored, then water from reservoirs alongside will fill the tube to bring the boat up to the height of the upper pound.

Barring any major setbacks, the Bedford Link is hoped to be operational by 2030.

Facts & Feats

Have you ever wondered which canal aqueduct is the longest? Or which canal locks are the deepest? Or which canal is the widest.

Here are a few facts that will either surprise you, impress your friends or may even come in handy down your local pub quiz!

The oldest man-made navigation in Britain is Fossdyke in Lincolnshire built by the Romans about 120 AD. Although passage was hampered in the 1600s due to poor maintenance, it has never closed.

One of the shortest-lived canals to cut a path through the English countryside was the 13-mile long Salisbury & Southampton Canal. Opened in 1802, it was abandoned just six years later.

The canal tunnel at Norwood was the first to measure over a mile in length. It took three years to complete and was lined with approximately three million bricks.

Even though the Thames & Medway Canal was only 6½ miles long, over two thirds of it passed through Strood Tunnel. Measuring nearly 2¼ miles, it was at one time the second longest in Britain!

For 22 years between 1789 and 1811, the record for the overall longest

tunnel in Britain was held by the 2¼ mile long Sapperton Canal Tunnel near Cirencester in Gloucestershire

At 3¼ miles, Standedge Tunnel has, since 1811, been the longest canal tunnel in Britain. Carrying the Huddersfield Narrow Canal beneath the southern reaches of the Pennines between Huddersfield and Manchester, it also holds the title of highest tunnel canal tunnel at 196 metres above sea level as well as the deepest at 194 metres below the surface.

The highest summit on any British man-made waterway was 645 feet above sea level along a 4-mile section between Diggle and Marsden on the Huddersfield Narrow Canal.

The longest aqueduct in England is situated near Bearley Cross on the Stratford-on-Avon Canal. Traversing road, rail and water meadows, it is 600 feet long with the tow path occupying its own trough alongside but below the waterline.

In November 1805, Thomas Telford's Pontcysyllte Aqueduct was opened after a decade in the making and at 1007 feet from end to end and 126 feet tall, remains to this day the longest and highest aqueduct in Britain.

Above: *Avon Aqueduct*

The Avon crossing at Falkirk on the Union Canal stands 86 feet above the river and measures 810 feet in length making it the highest and longest aqueduct in Scotland.

The Falkirk Wheel, opened in 2002 to reconnect the isolated Union Canal to the Forth & Clyde, weighs 1,200 tonnes. It is so finely balanced, however, that only 1.5KWh of electricity, the equivalent of boiling eight kettles is all it takes to rotate the two armatures. It cost £17.5 million to build.

At nearly 286½ miles long, the Grand Union is the longest canal in Britain with by far the most locks. At an average of almost one lock per mile, it has more than double the number of the next highest, the Kennet & Avon, with just over 100.

Throughout the history of British waterways, there have been several canals that, due in no small part to the terrain they were built to follow, had to include large concentrations of locks. For example, boats using the 30-mile Lichfield Canal, opened as early as 1797 but finally abandoned in 1955, were required to negotiate no fewer than 70 locks!

Between 1828 and 1910, the Liskeard & Looe Union meandered its weary way from one quaint Cornish town to another. It was built to only 6 miles in length, but any boatman attempting the journey was faced with 25 locks to contend with, averaging more than four per mile.

Yet the record for the ratio of most locks to overall canal length has to go to the Wardle. Built in 1829, it is shortest canal in Britain at just 154 feet, yet still manages to squeeze in a single lock, giving it an average of ten locks per mile – hypothetically speaking! The Wardle could hardly be described as a canal system, but is not simply a pointless stretch of water stuck in a field on its own. It performs an important role linking the Trent & Mersey to the Middlewich Branch of the Shropshire Union and forms a vital link in the popular Four Counties Ring (Shropshire, Staffordshire, Cheshire and West Midlands), a 110-mile round trip that many people successfully circumnavigate in a fortnight's boating holiday.

Far Left: *Wardle Canal*

Conversely, Bridgewater Canal had not a single lock to hamper progress along its 40 miles when it opened in 1761.

The highest concentration of locks in one place is in a 2-mile section of the Worcester & Birmingham Canal. Here, 36 locks in two flights allow narrow boats to descend a drop of 220 feet between the villages of Tardebigge and Stoke Prior.

The standard dimensions for a British canal lock are 70 feet long by 7 feet wide.

At a slender 5½ feet in width, the Bude Canal had the narrowest locks on any man-made commercial waterway in Britain.

The Manchester Ship Canal which had to be built 65 feet wide to enable large freight vessels to pass each other on their voyage between Merseyside and Salford.

The deepest locks in Britain, that is to say those that have the greatest

'rise' or difference between being full of water and empty, can be found on the Kennet & Avon Canal at Bath and on the Rochdale Canal at Sowerby Bridge. Both have a rise of 20 feet.

As regards the United Kingdom, the lock with the greatest rise is the Ardnacrusha Lock on the Shannon Navigation, Ireland where boats are lowered a total of 100 feet in two chambers that are linked via a tunnel.

The steepest lock staircase is Bingley Five-Rise which lifts the Leeds & Liverpool Canal 59 feet, over a distance of 320 feet, and at an angle of 1 in 5.

The longest working narrow boats were used on the rather more generously proportioned Wryley and Essington that connected with the Cannock Extension Canal and served collieries north of Wolverhampton. Measuring 85 feet in length and 8½ feet across the beam, they were unsuitable for any other system and when their commercial life was over, practically all were laid up and scrapped.

Right: *Vessels on the Grand Union Canal at Ventnor Farm*

ALSO AVAILABLE IN THE LITTLE BOOK SERIES

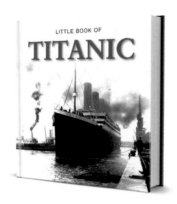

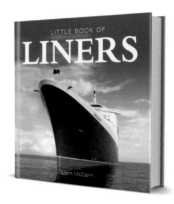

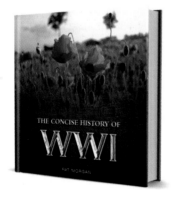

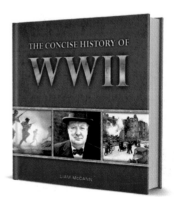